Flat Peyote - Even Count

If you are learning this stitch, you may want to make a small practice swatch.

Rows 1 and 2 -
String 10 beads, using a "stop" bead about 8" from the end of the thread. Use a different size

Stop Bead

or style bead, so you will not confuse it with the others. Alternate colors of beads, as shown in the diagram.

You can see on the diagrams that bead #1 matches the color of the beads in Row 2.

Row 3 -
String on bead 11, pass the needle through bead 9. (You are "skipping" bead 10, the last bead strung.) Continue to add beads 12 - 15.

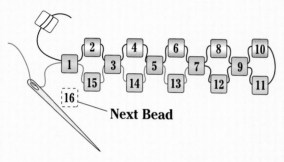

Next Bead

Row 4 -
Add bead 16, pass needle through bead 15. Tip: Hold the work carefully at this point, as you do not want the beads to twist out of position. Continue adding beads 17 through 20. Bead 20 is the last bead on Row 4.

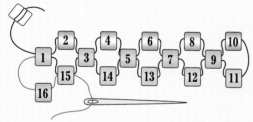

Row 5 -
Add bead 21, passing the needle through bead 20. Bead 21 is the first bead of Row 5.

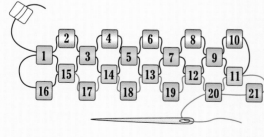

As you add the rest of the beads on Row 4, you will begin to see how the rows line up with each other, and how the beads fit into each other, like a zipper's teeth.

You will have "down" beads that you go into when adding the next row. If you are using cylinder beads, this will be even more apparent.

Flat Peyote - Odd Count

Odd Count Flat Peyote is worked just the same as even count, but one edge will be different.

If you are learning this stitch, make a small piece to practice this odd count edge turn-around.

Rows 1 and 2 -
String on 9 beads, using a stop bead and proceed as for Flat Peyote - Even Count through bead 13.

Row 3 -
From bead 13 go back through bead 2 and bead 1.

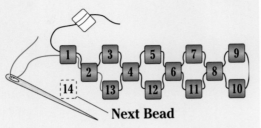

'Turn the Edge'

Row 4 -
String on bead 14 and go through bead 2 and bead 3, pull beads into place.

Row 5 -
Go through beads 13, 2, and 1, and back through bead 14. String on bead 15, go through bead 13 and proceed as usual.

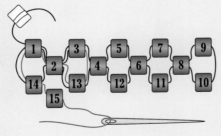

In Flat Peyote - Odd Count, one end will always be done the same way as Flat Peyote - Even Count.

The other end must be 'turned', as in Row 3 above, for the first row.

Thereafter, on the odd edge, "loop" around the thread as shown in the diagram.

As an option, you may continue any extra weaving at the odd edge.

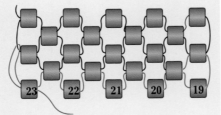

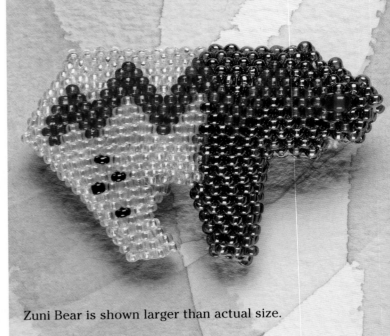

Zuni Bear is shown larger than actual size.

Zuni Bear

The bear is a symbol of strength and courage in Southwest design. The zig-zag lightning bolt symbolizes power and speed. Interpret your own bear design with your favorite colors.

SIZE: $1^{1}/2$" x $2^{1}/8$"
STITCHES:
Flat Peyote
MATERIALS:
8° or 11° seed beads:
☐ White AB
▨ Turquoise
▨ Root Bear
▨ Dark Blue
☐ Pink
8° seed beads:
⬭ Red
Beading supplies:
needle
thread

INSTRUCTIONS:
• Weave the bear body.
• Begin on the 'center' line. Work toward the head. When finished with the head half of the body, join a new thread through the 'center' line and work toward the legs and tail.
• Fold the bear in half.
• Join the edges around the first half of bear and stuff. Continue joining and stuffing until complete.
• Add a bead loop and key chain if desired.

Bear Body

'Center' Line
Begin Here

How to Join Rows of Beads

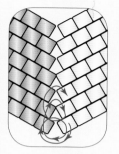

Side-by-Side Join

Many of these projects join with two rows of beads sitting side-by-side instead of 'zipping' the rows together.

Just weave back and forth between the rows of beads.

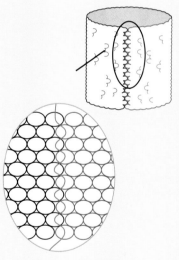

Zipper Join

Join a seam between two sides of Flat Peyote with a 'saw-tooth' or 'zipper' join.

Take your thread through the first end bead, and through the next bead that fits into the 'zipper' on the other side. Continue, pulling thread snug every 3 or 4 stitches. Don't pull too tightly or your work will warp.

Decrease Beads in a Row

1. Skip one bead on Row 1.

2. Add 2 beads in that space on Row 2.

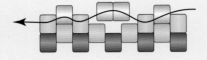

3. Add no bead on Row 3.

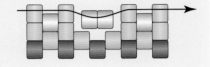

4. Add only 1 bead in that space on Row 4.

Increase Beads in a Row

1. Bead as usual.

2. On the next row, add 2 beads in one bead space.

3. On the next row, add 1 bead between the two beads.

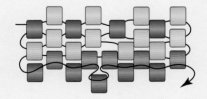

4. On the next row, add a bead in every space.

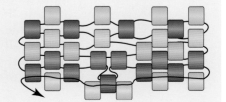

Purple Phoenix

Take a beading flight of royal fancy. This stunning purple Phoenix features exquisite tail feathers and a geometric body design in regal colors.

SIZE: 1¹/₂" x 4"
STITCHES:
  Flat Peyote & Fringe
MATERIALS:
11° seed beads:
☐ Pink
▨ Orchid
▩ Purple AB
☐ Pale Blue
Beading supplies:
  needle
  thread

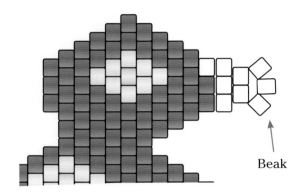

Beak

INSTRUCTIONS:
• **Body:** Weave one phoenix body.
• Begin on the 'center' line. Work toward the body. When finished with the body, join a new thread through the 'center' line and work toward the head.
• Stitch a second body.
• Join the edges halfway around and stuff. Continue joining and stuffing all the way around.
• **Wings:** Weave 2 wings. Sew both wings to the body.
• **Beak:** Join a new thread to the front of the head. Make the beak
• **Feet:** Join a new thread on the bottom of the body. Make the feet.
• **Tail:** Join a new thread to the back of the body. Add 6 long strips of fringe for tail feathers.
• Add a bead loop and key chain if desired.

Tail Fringe
Add 6

Phoenix is shown larger than actual size.

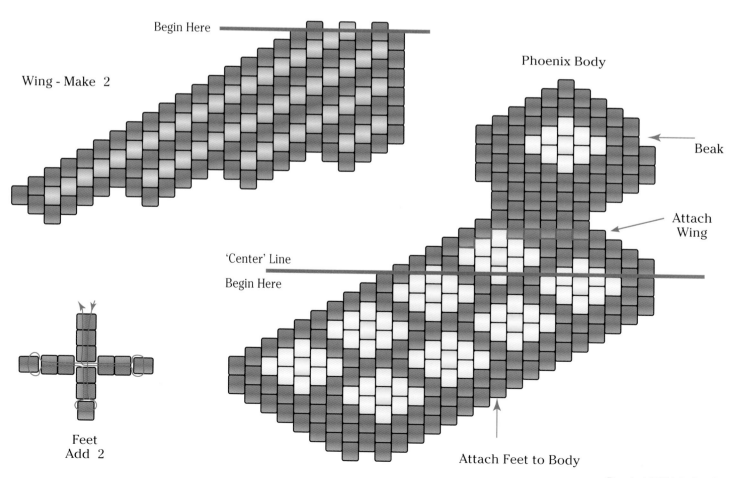

Wing - Make 2

Begin Here

Phoenix Body

Beak

Attach Wing

'Center' Line

Begin Here

Feet
Add 2

Attach Feet to Body

Small Butterfly

Your creative spirit will take flight with these colorful butterflies.

Give your beaded art new wings with this pretty project.

SIZE: 1¹/₂" x 2¹/₄"

STITCHES:
Flat Peyote & Fringe

MATERIALS:

11° seed beads:
- Black
- Silver Lined Gold
- Silver Lined Green
- Iridescent Cranberry
- Iridescent Pale Blue

Beading supplies:
 needle
 thread

INSTRUCTIONS:
- **Body**: Weave the body in a tube (page 9).
- Begin on the 'center' line. Work toward the head. When finished with this half, join a new thread through the 'center' line and work toward the tail. Decreasing beads will give the body a rounded shape.
- Draw up beads on the ends to close up any openings.
- **Wings**: Weave 2 wings.
- Sew both wings to the body.
- **Antennae**: Join a new thread to the head, then add the antenna.
- **Feet**: Join a new thread to the bottom, then add 6 feet.
- Add a bead loop and key chain if desired.

Butterflies are shown larger than actual size.

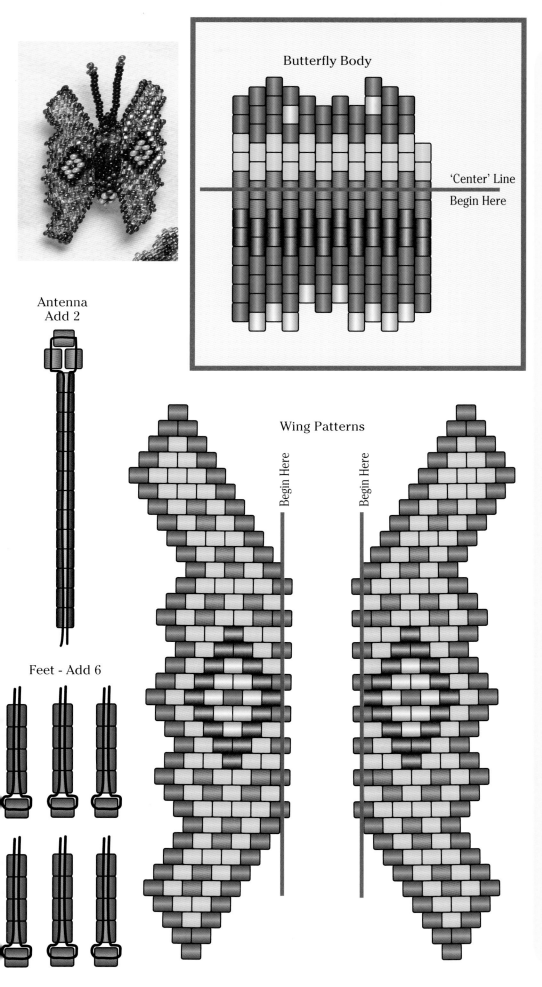

Butterfly Body

'Center' Line

Begin Here

Antenna
Add 2

Wing Patterns

Begin Here

Begin Here

Feet - Add 6

Work as in Flat Peyote.

String on the required number of beads. Tie in a circle, leaving one bead space so the tension will not be too tight as you work the next row.

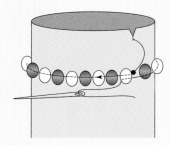

Stepping Down

Take the needle back through the 1st bead strung to position the thread for the next row.

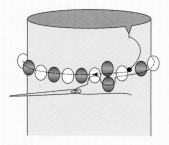

Step down. Take the needle back through the first bead in the row just completed. You must do this at the end of each row.

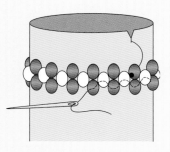

Work around a center to make it easier to hold the beads securely. Use a glass bottle, drinking straw or paper tube.

From tropical fish to sea animals, and domesticated cats to colorful fantasy birds, "Beaded Wild Animals" brings you a tempting array of beading experiences. These finished pieces make perfect pendants.

Hummingbird

This project will get your beading needle humming. Hummingbirds are named for the characteristic sound made by their wings. Distinguished by their ability to hover in mid-air, they are the only birds that can deliberately fly backwards.

Create your own beaded tribute to these tiny skilled fliers.

SIZE: 3" x 3 1/4"
STITCHES:
  Flat Peyote, Tubular Peyote & Fringe
MATERIALS:
11° seed beads:
☐ Silver Lined Teal
☐ Silver Lined Cobalt Blue
☐ Silver Lined Aqua
☐ Silver Lined Gold
☐ Black
☐ Iridescent Gray
☐ Iridescent Purple
☐ Yellow
☐ Red
▭▭▭▭▭ Iridescent Purple bugle bead

Beading supplies:
  needle
  thread

Hummingbirds are shown larger than actual size.

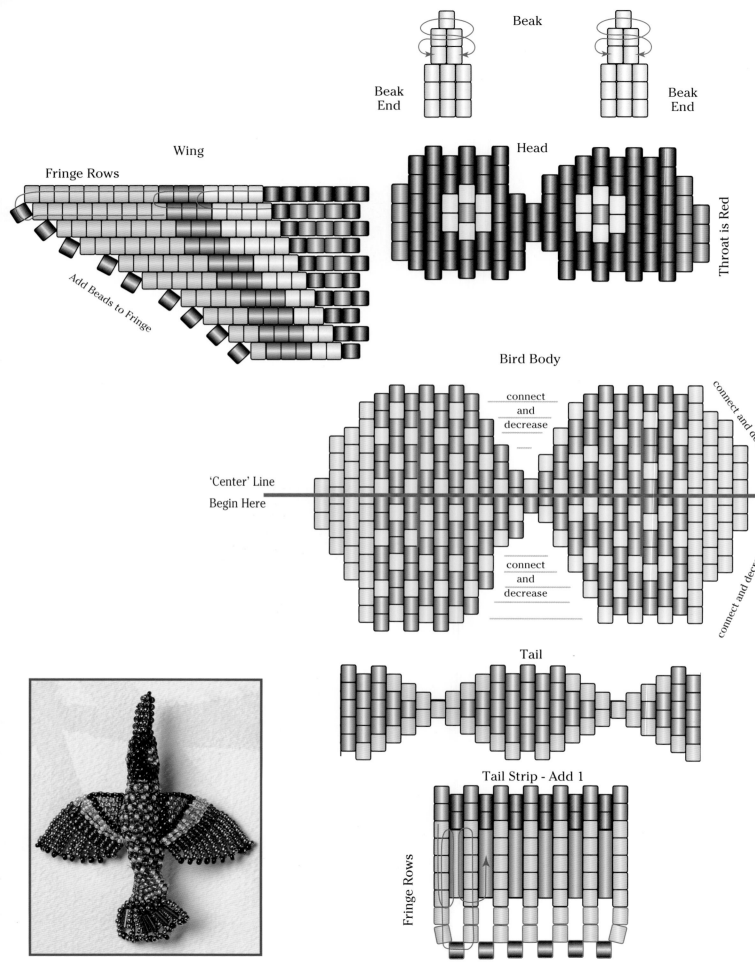

Beak

Beak
End

Beak
End

Head

Throat is Red

Wing

Fringe Rows

Add Beads to Fringe

Bird Body

connect
and
decrease

connect and decr

'Center' Line

Begin Here

connect
and
decrease

connect and decrease

Tail

Tail Strip - Add 1

Fringe Rows

Wing

Fringe Rows

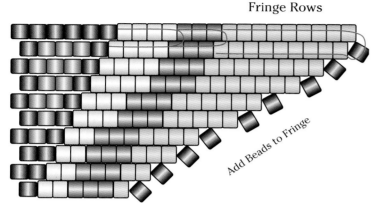

Add Beads to Fringe

Hummingbird

SIZE: 3" x 3¹/₄"

STITCHES:
Flat Peyote, Tubular
Peyote & Fringe

MATERIALS:

11° seed beads:
- Silver Lined Teal
- Silver Lined Cobalt Blue
- Silver Lined Aqua
- Silver Lined Gold
- Black
- Iridescent Gray
- Iridescent Purple
- Yellow
- Red
- Iridescent Purple bugle bead

Beading supplies:
needle
thread

INSTRUCTIONS:
- **Body**: Weave the bird body.
- Begin on the 'center' line. Work toward the head. Reduce stitches along the back and along the tummy of the bird to make a rounded shape.
- When finished with this half, join a new thread through the 'center' line and weave toward the tail (reducing stitches as before).
- Fold the body in half. Join the edges together beginning at the tail and stuff. Continue joining and stuffing. Leave the neck open.
- **Head**: Join a new thread at the neck. Stitch the head in a tube (page 9). Stuff. Stitch the mouth end closed.
- **Wings**: Join a new thread through the beads on the body where a wing will go, then weave the wing. Add additional rows for the fringe ends of the wings. Sew wing fringes to each other where the colors change.
- Join another thread and make the second wing.
- **Tail**: Join a thread to the back of body. Weave the tail piece as a tube (page 9) curving it to fit the body. Complete additional rows.
- Add additional rows for the fringe ends of the tail. Sew tail fringes to each other where the colors change.
- **Beak**: Join a thread then stitch the beak, working in a tube (page 9).
- Add a bead loop and key chain if desired.

Monarch butterflies are shown actual size.

Monarch Butterfly

His name means "king" and this gorgeous design lives up to its name. Monarch butterflies have a distinctive wing shape that is immediately recognizable. Enjoy one of nature's most regal inventions with these easy to bead patterns.

SIZE: 3" x 3 1/4"

STITCHES:
Flat Peyote & Fringe

MATERIALS:
11° seed beads:
▢ Black
☐ Silver Lined Clear
▢ Silver Lined Blue
▢ Silver Lined Green
☐ Silver Lined Gold
▢ Dark Blue AB
⬭ 8° E beads

Beading supplies:
needle
thread

Body

'Center' Line

Begin Here

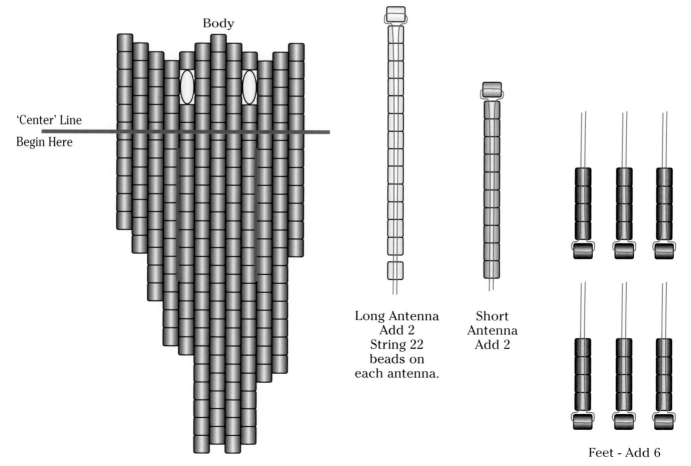

Long Antenna
Add 2
String 22
beads on
each antenna.

Short
Antenna
Add 2

Feet - Add 6

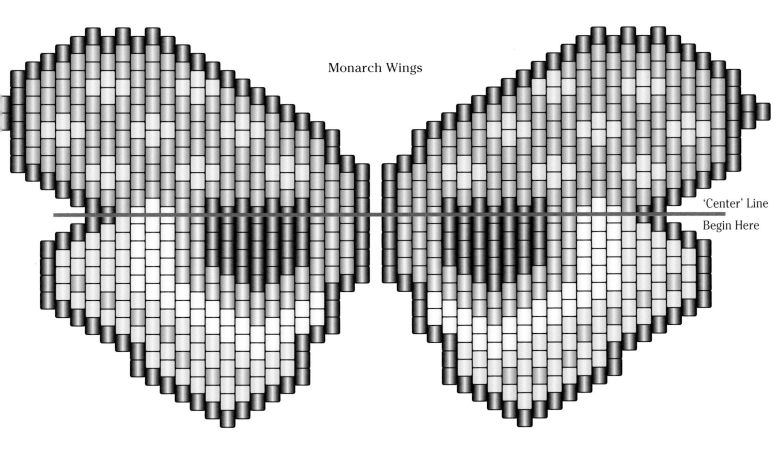

Monarch Wings

'Center' Line

Begin Here

SIZE: 3" x 3¼"

STITCHES:
  Flat Peyote
  & Fringe

MATERIALS:

11° seed beads:
▣ Black
☐ Silver Lined Clear
▣ Silver Lined Blue
▣ Silver Lined Green
▣ Silver Lined Gold
▣ Dark Blue AB
⬯   8° E beads

Beading supplies:
  needle
  thread

Monarch Butterfly

INSTRUCTIONS:
• **Body**: Weave the body.
• Begin on the 'center' line. Work toward the head When finished with this half, join a new thread through the 'center' line and work toward the tail
• Starting at one end, join the body into a tube.
• **Wings**: Weave 2 wings.
• Attach to body (as shown by red lines on the chart).
• **Antennae**: Join a new thread to add the antennae.
• **Feet**: Join a new thread to add 6 feet.
• Add a bead loop and key chain if desired.

Sea Turtle

Did you know that marine turtles are one of the Earth's most ancient creatures, with a fossil record going back 150 million years?

And, like people, all sea turtles have their own special faces! Capture the unique patterns and gorgeous colors of the Sea Turtle.

SIZE: 2³/₈" x 2³/₄"

STITCHES:
  Flat Peyote,
  Tubular Peyote & Fringe

MATERIALS:

11° seed beads:
☐ Black
☐ Red
☐ Iridescent Caramel
☐ Iridescent Light Green
☐ Iridescent White
☐ Iridescent Sand
☐ Brown metallic

Beading supplies:
  needle
  thread

Turtles are shown larger than actual size.

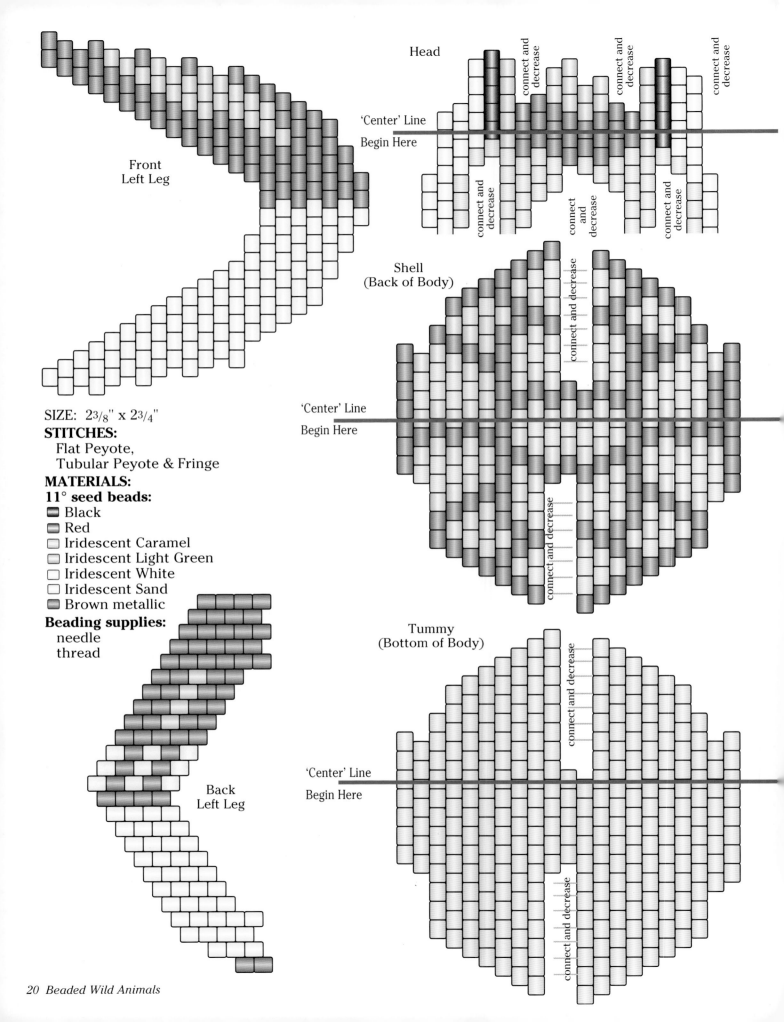

Front
Left Leg

Head

connect and decrease

connect and decrease

connect and decrease

connect and decrease

'Center' Line

Begin Here

connect and decrease

connect and decrease

connect and decrease

Shell
(Back of Body)

connect and decrease

'Center' Line

Begin Here

connect and decrease

SIZE: 2³/₈" x 2³/₄"
STITCHES:
   Flat Peyote,
   Tubular Peyote & Fringe
MATERIALS:
11° seed beads:
   Black
   Red
   Iridescent Caramel
   Iridescent Light Green
   Iridescent White
   Iridescent Sand
   Brown metallic
Beading supplies:
   needle
   thread

Back
Left Leg

Tummy
(Bottom of Body)

connect and decrease

'Center' Line

Begin Here

connect and decrease

INSTRUCTIONS:
- **Body:** Weave the body.
- Begin on the 'center' line. Work toward the head. When finished with this half, join a new thread through the 'center' line and work toward the tail. Decreasing beads will make the tummy rounded.
- Fold the body in half. Leave the neck and tail open. Join the body halfway down the back and stuff. Continue joining and stuffing.
- **Tail:** Join a new thread around the tail opening. Weave the tail as a tube (page 9). Stuff as you go.
- When you reach the bottom of the 'tail', decrease 4 beads and begin weaving the 'tail extension'. Continue weaving in a tube to the end of the tail. Curl and sew the tip of the tail to the middle of the tail.
- **Head:** Join a new thread at the neck. Weave the head in a tube (page 9). Leave the nose open. Stuff as you stitch. Decreasing beads will make the head rounded.
- **Crests:** Join a new thread. Add five 3-bead spikes along the back.
- **Nose:** Stitch and join into tube. Sew to head.
- **Ears:** Join a new thread to the body. Weave the ears.
- **Fins:** Join new threads to stitch the fins.

Tail Extension

connect and decrease

- **Extend Stripes:** Join a new thread. Add beads to sides of body to extend stripes. Refer to photo for placement
- Add a bead loop and key chain if desired.

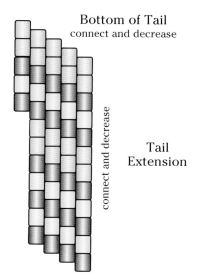

Bottom of Tail
connect and decrease

connect and decrease

Tail Extension

Seahorse

SIZE: 1" x 3³/₄"

STITCHES:
Flat Peyote & Tubular Peyote

MATERIALS:

11° seed beads:
- ☐ Lavender
- ☐ Cranberry AB
- ☐ Silver Lined Yellow
- 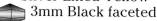 3mm Black faceted

Beading supplies:
needle
thread

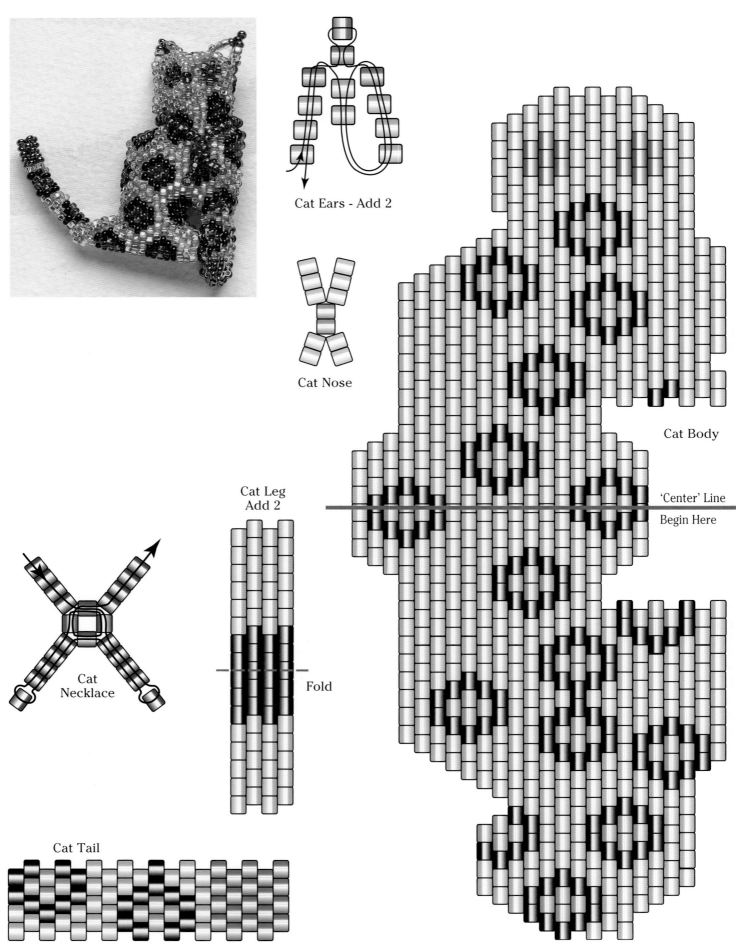

Cat Ears - Add 2

Cat Nose

Cat Body

'Center' Line

Begin Here

Cat Leg
Add 2

Fold

Cat
Necklace

Cat Tail

Clever Cats

The ancient Egyptians worshiped cats. Today, many share a deep fondness for these entertaining and often cryptic felines.

These beaded designs bring to life many characteristics that are unique to these purr-fect pals.

SIZE: 2" x 2¼"

STITCHES:
Flat Peyote
Tubular Peyote

MATERIALS:
11° seed beads:
❏ Silver Lined Gold
❏ Silver Lined Blue
❏ Silver Lined Root Beer
❏ Silver Lined Green
❏ Silver Lined Red
❏ Black
❏ Pink Lined Clear
❏ Brown Metallic

Beading supplies:
needle
thread

INSTRUCTIONS:
• **Body:** Weave the cat body.
• Begin on the 'center' line working toward the head. When finished with this half, join a new thread through the 'center' line and work toward the tail.
• Fold the body in half. Leave the tail open. Join the body halfway around and stuff. Continue joining and stuffing all the way around.
• **Tail:** Join a new thread at the tail. Stitch the tail in a tube (page 9).
• **Ears:** Join a new thread to stitch the ears.
• **Nose:** Add the nose.
• **Legs:** Stitch the leg strips in a tube (page 9). Sew legs to the body.
• **Necklace:** Make a necklace and sew it to the cat.
• Add a bead loop and key chain if desired.

Cats are shown larger than actual size.

Big Fish

"I caught one this BIG!" Even if it's just a fish story, bead a design to commemorate your adventures with line and lure.

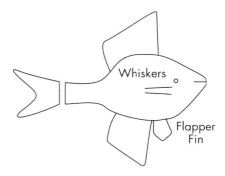

SIZE: 2¹/₂" x 3¹/₄"
STITCHES:
  Flat Peyote & Fringe Rows
MATERIALS:
11° seed beads:
▨ Silver Lined Red
☐ Silver Lined Gold
▨ Silver Lined Green
☐ Silver Lined Turquoise
▨ Black
▨ Cobalt Blue
Beading supplies:
  needle
  thread

Big Fish are shown larger than actual size.

Big Fish

SIZE: 2¹/₂" x 3¹/₄"

STITCHES:
  Flat Peyote & Fringe Rows

MATERIALS:

11° seed beads:
  ▢ Silver Lined Red
  ▢ Silver Lined Gold
  ▢ Silver Lined Green
  ▢ Silver Lined Turquoise
  ▢ Black
  ▢ Cobalt Blue

Beading supplies:
  needle
  thread

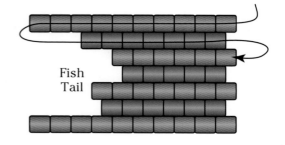

Fish Tail

INSTRUCTIONS:
• **Body:** Weave the fish body.
• Begin on the 'center' line. Work toward the top half of the body. When finished with this half, join a new thread through the 'center' line and work toward the bottom half.
• Fold the body in half. Join the body halfway around and stuff. Continue joining and stuffing all the way around.
• **Tail:** Join a new thread at the tail. Stitch the tail in rows.
• **Top Fin:** Join a new thread at the top of the back. Stitch the top fin in rows.
• **Bottom Fin:** Join a new thread at the bottom. Stitch the bottom fin in rows.
• **Flapper Fins:** Join new threads. Stitch the flapper fins in rows.
• **Whiskers:** Join new threads. Stitch the whiskers in rows.
• Add a bead loop and key chain if desired.

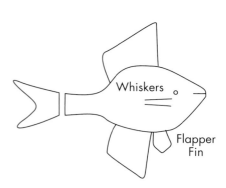

Whiskers

Flapper Fin